WALKS FOR
ALL AGES

SURREY

CHRIS HOWARD

BRADWELL
BOOKS

Published by Bradwell Books
11 Orgreave Close Sheffield S13 9NP
Email: books@bradwellbooks.co.uk

British Library Cataloguing in Publication Data: a catalogue record for this book is available from the British Library.

1st Edition
ISBN: 9781912060665
Design by: Andy Caffrey
Typesetting and mapping: Mark Titterton
Photograph credits: the author, her friends (credited where known) and iStock
Print: Gomer Press, Llandysul, Ceredigion SA44 4JL

Maps: Contain Ordnance Survey data
© Crown copyright and database right 2018
Ordnance Survey licence number 100039353

The information in this book has been produced in good faith and is intended as a general guide. Although the maps in this book are based on original Ordnance Survey (OS) mapping, walkers are always advised to use a detailed OS map. Look in 'The Basics' section for recommendations for the most suitable map for each of the walks.

Bradwell Books and the authors have made all reasonable efforts to ensure that the details are correct at the time of publication. Bradwell Books and the authors cannot accept responsibility for any changes that have taken place subsequent to the book being published.

It is the responsibility of individuals undertaking any of the walks listed in this book to exercise due care and consideration for their own health and well-being and that of others in their party. The walks in this book are not especially strenuous, but individuals taking part should ensure they are fit and well before setting off.

A good pair of walking books is essential for these walks. It is advisable to take good-quality waterproofs, and if undertaking the walks during the winter, take plenty of warm clothing as well. Because the walks will take some time, it would be a good idea to take along some food and drink.

Enjoy walking. Enjoy Surrey with Bradwell Books!

CONTENTS

INTRODUCTION

Surrey, being one of the Home Counties, is often misconceived as a leafy outpost of London. Nothing could be further from the truth. The London Greenbelt legislation and the designation of the Surrey Hills as an Area of Outstanding Natural Beauty (AONB) on 8 May 1958 has meant much of Surrey remains as it has been for over a thousand years, with rolling chalk hills, rare lowland heaths, farms and woodlands.

The easy access from London by train from Victorian times has meant that the county has been a popular place to live for commuters ever since. It was a favourite spot for the London Victorians to come for their leisure time as well as becoming a mecca for cycling, a link that was reinforced in 2012 when London and Surrey played host to the Olympic cycle race and people from all around the world watched the men and women's events with their circuits of Box Hill, one of the most visited natural sites in the South of England.

Interestingly, however, one of the most beautiful valleys in Surrey, the Tillingbourne, was known from Tudor times as one of the county's most industrial regions. The many mills that sat along the river churned out not only basics such as flour but also sinister things like gunpowder and even French money, destined for France in a bid to undermine the Napoleonic Empire. You can still see the remains of this fascinating industry, as described in the Chilworth walk (Walk 6)

INTRODUCTION

Being so close to London, Surrey has always been a playground for the rich and famous. Originally, it was the kings and queens of England, who had many hunting lodges and palaces in the county. Later it was the Victorians who built their wonderful legacy of Arts and Crafts houses in the area. Today, the modern-day rich and famous enjoy a rural lifestyle while still being less than an hour from two major international airports and, of course, London.

One of the most internationally famous sites is the Runnymede fields, within sight of Windsor Castle on the River Thames. This is where King John was forced to sign the famous legal document, the Magna Carta, which is recognised as an important starting point for the progress of modern democracy.

Surrey is a walkers' paradise. It contains one of the most comprehensive networks of bridleways and footpaths in the country. Surprisingly, it is also the most densely wooded county in England. One of its best-kept secrets is the North Downs Way (NDW) national trail, designated in 1958. It is also associated with the Pilgrims' Way, familiar from Chaucer's *Canterbury Tales*. The NDW is an outstanding walking route, which enters the county at Farnham and crosses right through the middle of the Surrey Hills AONB before passing through the Kent Downs via Canterbury to Dover.

I am sure you will enjoy each and every walk in this book, all of which have been specially chosen to highlight some of the hidden gems of Surrey, while providing a free and enjoyable day out for the whole family – both two and four-legged!

1 GUILDFORD

THIS IS AN EASY TWO-MILE WALK AROUND THIS HISTORIC MARKET TOWN, ONLY 40 MINUTES FROM CENTRAL LONDON BY TRAIN AND NESTLING IN THE NORTH DOWNS ON THE RIVER WEY. IT IS THE FINAL RESTING PLACE OF AUTHOR LEWIS CARROLL AND BOASTS AN ATTRACTIVE COBBLED HIGH STREET WITH A DISTINCTIVE 17TH-CENTURY TOWN CLOCK AND A NORMAN CASTLE RUIN AND GARDENS WITH VIEWS OVER THE SURREY HILLS.

This short, town and park walk showcases some of the best parts of Guildford. It boasts many famous residents, including the author of *Alice in Wonderland* as well as George Abbot, a 17th-century Archbishop of Canterbury, who created an almshouse or 'hospital', called Abbot's Hospital, that is still functioning to this day. The town straddles the River Wey and is surrounded by the Surrey Hills Area of Outstanding Natural Beauty (AONB).

Often mistakenly called a city, Guildford is one of the county's main market towns. With impressive castle ruins dating back to Norman times, the town became a successful trading centre due to the gap in the North Downs and the ease of navigation to London along the River Wey. Surrey's county town, Kingston-upon-Thames, is no longer actually situated within the county, having been swallowed up by Greater London in the rearrangement of boundaries in 1965. Many people consequently mistake Guildford for the county town, although the modern, thrusting Woking and centrally located Dorking also vie for this title.

Guildford has remained an attractive town despite several attempts by engineers and avant-garde architects to drive large highways and modern town developments through it in the 1960s and 70s. The streets are still largely laid out on medieval origins. The cobbled setts of the High Street and the large 1683 clock tower also help to maintain its old-world charm. The views to the open countryside of the Surrey Hills add to the attractiveness of this town.

The River Wey is a central feature of the town, eventually joining the River Thames at Weybridge. The Wey Navigations date from 1653, being one of the first navigable river systems in England. In 1816 the Wey and Arun Junction Canal was opened, linking to the south coast via the Arun Navigation. Conceived during the Napoleonic Wars, the canal

was intended to provide a safe, efficient route from London to Portsmouth to carry goods supplying the dockyards.

The golden sand at the footbridge over the River Wey is on the ancient Pilgrims' Way – a long-distance walking route to Canterbury Cathedral. Some people believe this is how Guildford got its name, the 'guild' meaning gold and 'ford' referring to the shallow crossing over the river.

The town also features an attractive Norman castle ruin. Guildford Castle is thought to have been built shortly after the 1066 invasion of England by William the Conqueror. It fell into disrepair in the 14th century. Since Victorian times the grounds have been an attractive pleasure garden.

George Abbot (1562–1633) was born in Guildford and became Archbishop of Canterbury in 1611. Guildford remembers him with a statue in the High Street, a pub and also a secondary school named after him.

THE BASICS

Distance: 2 miles / 3.2km

Gradient: Easy walk on tarmac paths, although Guildford is built on the side of a hill

Severity: Easy

Approx. time to walk: 1½ hours but allow longer as there is so much to stop and see

Stiles: None

Maps: OS Landranger 186 (Aldershot & Guildford); OS Explorer 145 (Guildford & Farnham)

Path description: Flat tarmac paths. Cobbled setts of the High Street are slightly uneven

Start point: Tunsgate Arch, junction of High Street and Tunsgate (GR SU 997494)

Parking: There are several pay and display multi-storey car parks in the town centre and an excellent park and ride service

Dog friendly: Yes, but will need to be on a lead in the town due to the busy roads

Public toilets: There are several public toilets in the town, in Tunsgate and North Street, as well as in the many pubs and cafes in the town

Nearest food: Guildford has a wide variety of cafes, restaurants and pubs to choose from. It also has an excellent tourist office in the High Street in Guildford House to assist you

1 GUILDFORD WALK

THE ROUTE

1. Start in the town centre, at Tunsgate Arch, which was built in 1818 as the portico for the town's Corn Exchange. Opposite is the Guildhall which dates from the 14th century. It houses an impressive town clock dating from 1683. Walk up Tunsgate to view the Norman castle. Cross over Castle Street and through the gates, to the Bowling Green.

2. The Castle Grounds and Bowling Green were bought by Guildford Corporation in 1885. They were laid out as pleasure gardens to celebrate Queen Victoria's Golden Jubilee in 1888. Follow the path around the Bowling Green, and then down into the lower gardens at the base of the castle keep.

3. Turn left past some of the remains of the Royal Palace, now set amongst award-winning gardens, and go through the arch on the left.

4. Turn left and follow the path to an iron gate on your right after 25 yards.

5. In this garden you will see a statue of *Alice Through the Looking Glass*, created in memory of Lewis Carroll, who lived in the large house nearby called The Chestnuts until his death in 1871. He wrote much of this second book about Alice here.

6. Retrace your steps and follow the path, which joins a road down to the Castle Arch. The arch was built in 1256, as the main entrance to Guildford Castle. Turn right into Quarry Street, past Guildford Museum, and down to St Mary's Church, the only remaining building in Guildford dating from the Saxon period.

7. Turn left into Mill Lane and cross over at the traffic lights. Walk past the old mill used for milling corn and pumping the water supply. Walk along the alley to the left of the Yvonne Arnaud Theatre (opened in 1965) to the Wey Navigation.

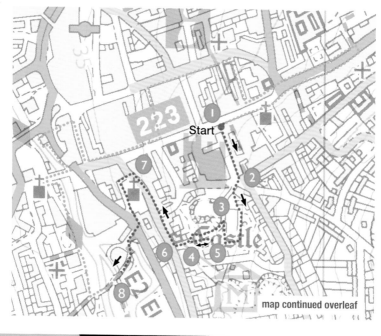

Start

223

map continued overleaf

8. Cross over the canal and the river to Millmead and turn right at the car park and walk along the river until you see an attractive statue of *Alice in Wonderland*, showing Alice with her sister and the White Rabbit. Continue on until you come to the Town Bridge.

9. Turn right over the bridge to look back up the attractive High Street. Turn immediately left and follow the river path. Note the statue on the left of *The Bargeman*, which recognises the long history of trading on this river. Look out for an underpass on your right, just before the next bridge, called Friary Passage.

10. Go up Friary Passage to Friary Square. The Friary Shopping Centre opposite takes its name from the medieval Dominican Friary that used to stand on the site. The site later became the site of the Friary Brewery.

11. Turn right and walk down Friary Street to the High Street. Turn left up the High Street. You will pass the attractive Angel Hotel, the last surviving Georgian coaching inn in the town. In Georgian times, Guildford was a convenient halfway point between London and the South Coast. The Angel itself dates from medieval times. It has been an inn since 1522.

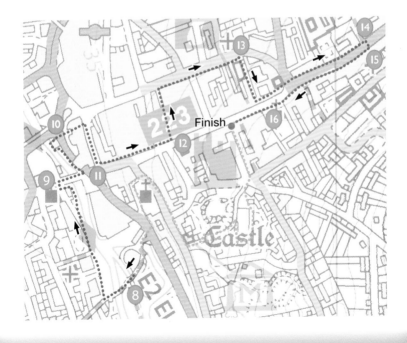

12. Turn left along Angel Gate and turn right into North Street. At the top of the hill you come to Quaker's Acre, originally the Town's old Quaker burial ground. The public toilet opposite under the clock tower was once Guildford's first fire station, opened in 1872.

13. A little further up, just past the Library, turn right into Jefferies Passage and re-join the High Street. Directly opposite is Holy Trinity Church. This Georgian church was rebuilt in 1761 after the original spire collapsed during building alterations. Opposite the church stands Abbot's Hospital, founded in 1619 by George Abbot, a local Guildfordian who became Archbishop of Canterbury. Further up the High Street is a statue of George Abbot.

14. Continue on into the Upper High Street to the Royal Grammar School. It was built in 1553, when Edward VI re-endowed the school.

15. A little further up the High Street is the Grade I listed Somerset House. This building was originally built as a town house for the Duke of Somerset, who used to stay here on his way to his estate at Petworth in West Sussex.

16. Go back down the High Street to the start of the walk, visiting Guildford House, on the right, as you go. This is now a gallery and tourist office and is free to enter. It is a fine example of an Elizabethan town house. It was built for lawyer and Mayor of Guildford, John Childs, in 1660. It has been used as the Town's public art gallery since 1959.

2 LIGHTWATER COUNTRY PARK

THIS DELIGHTFUL, SHORT, HEATH AND WOODLAND WALK, WITH PICNIC AREA AND PLAYGROUND, IS A MUST FOR FAMILIES – BOTH TWO AND FOUR-LEGGED. THE PARK IS AN IMPORTANT FRAGMENT OF THE ONCE VAST BAGSHOT HEATH.

This is an easy walk, with good facilities, including toilets, picnic areas, a café and children's playground. A short climb towards the end of the walk will be rewarded with fabulous views over to London and Wembley Stadium.

The area extends to 59 hectares of predominantly heathland habitat but there are also ponds, woodland, meadows and areas of scrub. The Country Park area has a recorded history going back to Saxon times. The main road linking Chertsey Abbey and Frimley Priory skirted the base of High Curley Hill. The area was called *whit heke mere* (white, clear water, surrounded by grass), probably a reference to Hammond's Pond, and the source of the name of the nearby village of Lightwater. The top of High Curley is one of the highest points in Surrey.

The heathlands here offer the opportunity to observe a wide variety of wildlife, birds, mammals, plants and insects. The area has been designated a Site of Special Scientific Interest (SSSI) and is a haven for rare heathland species including birds like the Dartford warbler, the nightjar and stonechat. It is also home to the elusive sand lizard, which needs sunny, sheltered patches of bare sandy ground as found on drier heaths. If you go quietly, you may also be rewarded with a siting of a deer. Snakes, including the poisonous adder, are found on the Common. If walking through the heather on a warm day, watch out for adders basking in the sun!

During the summer the Country Park regularly has goats grazing in the area. They are on loan from the Surrey Wildlife Trust as part of a conservation programme. The goats graze on the gorse and scrub to help maintain the open nature of the heathland and its associated wildlife.

An adventure playground, suitable for children aged from toddlers to twelve-year-olds, is sited here. There is an excellent café which welcomes both children and dogs. There are public toilets and several areas with picnic tables.

The Park is well signposted from Junction 3 of the M3 motorway between the villages of Bagshot and Lightwater. From Guildford and Bracknell it is signed off the A322.

THE BASICS

Distance: 2 miles / 3.2 km

Gradient: Easy walk but one steep hill with steps to the summit

Severity: Easy to moderate

Approx. time to walk: Allow about 1½ hours

Stiles: None

Maps: OS Landranger 186 (Aldershot & Guildford); OS Explorer 145 (Guildford & Farnham)

Path description: Woodlands; paths can be a bit uneven. Watch out for trip hazards like tree roots

Start point: Lightwater Country Park car park, The Avenue, Lightwater, (GR SU 917621)

Parking: Large free car park at Lightwater Country Park (near GU18 5YL)

Dog friendly: Yes, but dog walkers should note that due to the ground-nesting birds in the heath, dogs are to be kept on leads from 1 March to 31 July

Public toilets: In the park near the café

Nearest food: The Lightwater Café in the Park. It has a great space for children, with a book and games corner. Also caters for dogs

THE ROUTE

1. Park at the café car park, if possible (other car parking is available). Walk towards the café and then bear left and left again at the toilets, picking up the purple signposts.

2. At the T-junction with the main entrance road, cross over and pick up the next purple post running along woodland near to the road. This takes you up to the main car park at the Leisure Centre. Cross the car park and pick up the purple posts from here. The path gradually ascends upwards.

3. Take the set of steep wooden stairs when they come up on your right. At the top of the steep incline you will reach High Curley, where you will be rewarded with fantastic views towards London. You can see the arch of Wembley Stadium and the BT (Post Office) Tower in the distance.

4. Turn left at the top, past the toposcope (indicating positions of local landmarks), and follow the purple posts down the hill on the other side through the woodland. Follow this path until you meet the M3 motorway running parallel on your left. Keep looking out for the purple signpost, which after a short distance will direct you to the right.

5. Turn right following the purple signposts across open heathland, where you will eventually come to a T-junction.

6. Turn left following the now purple and brown signpost, along a path that runs parallel to the Lightwater Leisure Centre sports fields on your right. At the end of these fields is a car park and the purple posts will indicate right. Walk along this road, which skirts the bottom of the playing fields until you spot the café again where you began.

3 GATTON PARK

THIS IS A SHORT, TWO-MILE WALK AROUND A GORGEOUS HISTORIC LANDSCAPE, DESIGNED BY CAPABILITY BROWN, NEAR REIGATE, THAT WAS ONCE OWNED BY THE FAMILY THAT INVENTED COLMAN'S MUSTARD.

The grounds at Gatton Park are gradually being restored to their former glory by the Gatton Trust and the National Trust, who share ownership of the estate. The park at Gatton is most famous for the work that was carried out between 1762 and 1766 by the famous English landscape designer Lancelot 'Capability' Brown. He was enlisted to work on the park by Sir James Colebrooke, who purchased Gatton in 1751. While there had been a park at Gatton from the mid-15th century onwards, Brown's work has proved to be the most enduring. He swept away the formal landscape that had previously been there and replaced it with informal naturalistic plantings which accentuated the rolling landscape of the park.

Gatton Park Estate was bought by Jeremiah Colman (of mustard fame) in 1888. He was also a passionate gardener. The estate was one of Capability Brown's most expensive commissions and Gatton Park and the National Trust have received Heritage Lottery Funds to re-landscape some of the park, back to Brown's original design.

The park at Gatton is approximately 600 acres in size. Of these, 260 are managed by the Gatton Trust, including the core features and gardens, and have limited access. The remaining 340 acres are owned by the National Trust and are made up of mixed woodlands and open parkland. This part of the park has open access all year round. The Gatton Trust does, however, open the interesting Japanese and alpine rock gardens to the public on a regular basis. There is also a popular family fair in the grounds each July.

The Royal Alexandra and Albert School is a co-educational boarding school. The Royal Alexandra and Albert School Act of 1949 united The Royal Alexandra School, which was founded in 1758, and The Royal Albert Orphan School, which was founded in 1864 as a national memorial to Prince Albert, the late husband of Queen Victoria. It is one of 36 state-maintained boarding schools in England and Wales, and one of the few state schools to educate children from primary school years to the sixth form.

There is a stone circle that you will pass on the walk, which was placed at Gatton Park by the Jerusalem Trust to commemorate the millennium. Each stone represents 200 years of time and is inscribed with quotes and poems of each era. The Park is well known for its excellent displays of snowdrops in February and its native British bluebell display in May.

THE BASICS

Distance: 2 miles / 3.2km

Gradient: Some undulating gentle hills and a steep climb back to the car park at the end of the walk

Severity: Moderate

Approx. time to walk: 1½ hours

Stiles: None

Maps: OS Landranger 187 (Dorking & Reigate); OS Explorer 146 (Dorking, Box Hill & Reigate)

Path description: This walk follows wide public footpaths across private, public and National Trust land. Can be very muddy in the winter

Start point: Reigate Hill car park, Wray Lane (GR TQ 262523), just south of Junction 8 of the M25

Parking: Reigate Hill car park (free), Wray Lane (RH2 0HX)

Dog friendly: Yes. Dogs are welcome in Gatton Park, but please keep them on leads as sheep are often grazing in the fields and there are lots of geese and ducks on the lake

Public toilets: In the car park

Nearest food: Reigate Hill Café is next to the car park. The Yew Tree traditional Inn is a short drive away and dates back to 1841

3 GATTON PARK WALK

THE ROUTE

1. The walk starts from Reigate Hill's Wray Lane car park. Enter Gatton Park, using the path marked with the National Trust sign, located opposite the Wray Lane car park entrance. At the first 'Discover Gatton' way marker post, head down the slope. This was the park's original carriage drive.

2. At the second post, take the left fork in the path.

3. Very shortly after the second post you will find the third post, situated above a viewpoint giving you a first glimpse of the historic Gatton Park.

4. Continue along the old carriage road to the fourth post, near a yew tree, and follow the arrow.

5. At the end of this path you will see Tower Lodge on your left, marking another of the entrances into the park. This lodge is made from local Gatton stone. Turn right at the fifth post.

6. Enjoy further views across the parkland and then you will spot the stone circle. Continue on to the sixth post, which points you right, down the hill towards Hop Garden Pond and through the open parkland.

7. Cross the open parkland and re-enter the woodland fringe to post seven. Take a sharp right up the steep bank into Nut Wood. As you reach the top of this path you will be rewarded by a picturesque view of the main lake, over the tops of the trees bordering the Serpentine. Once the path levels out, continue until you arrive at a junction of paths.

8. Take the path to the right. Continue, passing Wingate Hill. This offers a last opportunity to look back on the parkland. This is also a good place to try and spot the spire of St Andrew's Church nestling in the trees. The present building dates from the 16th century, but there has been a church on the site since at least Norman times.

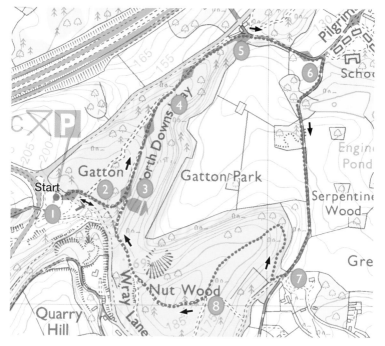

9. You will find post nine at the top of this slope. Turn right and head back to post three and the first viewpoint. At post three, follow the arrow left, taking you the short distance back to Wray Lane car park.

4 SHERE

THIS WALK TAKES IN THE BEAUTIFUL AND POPULAR VILLAGE OF SHERE, ONE OF THE TILLINGBOURNE VALLEY'S BEST-PRESERVED HISTORIC VILLAGES. THE WALK INCLUDES A TOUR OF THE VILLAGE, AS WELL AS A GENTLE STROLL OUT INTO THE SURROUNDING COUNTRYSIDE TO DISCOVER AN UNUSUAL AND UNUSED APOSTOLIC CHURCH AS WELL AS A RARE SURVIVING EXAMPLE OF A SAXON CHURCH, WHICH WAS USED IN THE 1994 FILM FOUR WEDDINGS AND A FUNERAL.

Shere was a wealthy village in medieval times, growing rich on the sought-after, hard-wearing woollen cloth the area produced. The water from the Tillingbourne was an important power source for the industry, using the mill to pound the cloth to thicken it, a process known as fulling.

The picturesque St James's Church, in the centre of the village, has been used for several films including *Four Weddings and a Funeral* and *Bridget Jones*. It was built in around 1190 in the transitional style and possibly built over an earlier church.

The White Horse pub (formally Cripps) was built in c. 1450 and is one of the oldest buildings in the village, the other being Forge Cottage. 'The Old Prison' in Lower Street dates from the 17th century, with its front wing said to have been used as the local lock-up.

The Catholic Apostolic Church and Chapterhouse is a Grade II* listed building on the outskirts of Shere, near Albury. It was built in 1840 by the architect William MacIntosh Brookes and paid for by local landowner, Henry Drummond. The church was administered by a college of twelve 'apostles' but was closed upon the death of the last minister, as the group had not made provision for ways to elect new apostles upon the original's deaths. The church is closed to the public.

The Bray family own much of the land around Shere and have done so for over 500 years, making it one of the oldest family estates in the country. The William Bray pub is named after a member of this family. In 2007, a previously unknown William Bray diary, covering 1754 and 1755, when he was aged just 18 or 19, was found in a garden shed. It is a fascinating document for many reasons. On Easter Monday 1755 he recorded playing a game of baseball, somewhere near Guildford, with a group of friends. This is particularly interesting because it is the earliest known manuscript reference to baseball, something some Americans are not too happy about!

There is a little museum in Shere, which is well worth a visit, and is open most weekends. It was originally the Working Men's Club, given to the veterans of World War I when the new Memorial Hall was built next door.

THE BASICS

Distance: 3 miles / 5 km

Gradient: Easy walk with one moderate hill to climb

Severity: Easy to moderate. Woodland paths can be a bit uneven. Watch out for trip hazards such as tree roots

Approx. time to walk: 2½ hours but allow longer as there is so much to stop and see

Stiles: None

Maps: OS Landranger 186 (Aldershot & Guildford); OS Explorer 145 (Guildford & Farnham)

Path description: Variety of footpaths, lanes and country footpaths, some next to the river

Start point: Shere Village car park (GR TQ 074479)

Parking: Shere Village car park which is very popular, so get there early (GU5 9HE)

Dog friendly: Yes, but look out for livestock in the fields

Public toilets: In the old fire station on Middle Street and in the two pubs

Nearest food: Shere is well provided for with the White Horse and William Bray pubs and the Dabbling Duck tea room as well as a wonderful ice cream shop selling locally made ice cream and chocolate

4 SHERE WALK

THE ROUTE

1. From the car park, turn left and cross the road towards Middle Street, the main street in Shere. Pass the 18th-century well, which was gifted to the village by two local sisters who wished there to be a non-alcoholic alternative to the village pubs for visitors.

2. Turn right down Lower Street, following the stream to the road's corner junction. Look out for the interesting old prison building (now a house) on your left, opposite the attractive allotments. Turn right at the junction, cross over the ford and follow the path up the incline until you reach a house on your left.

3. Turn left onto the footpath running beside the house and garden wall. Keep straight ahead on this path until you reach a field. Go through the gate and follow the path over the field to the far left corner, where you will see a kissing gate. Go through the gate and into the woods.

4. Keep straight ahead through the wood and out into another open field. You will come across the attractive Apostolic Church. With the church on your left, keep straight ahead until you reach a kissing gate.

5. Go through the kissing gate and you will then meet the A248 road. Turn left here and walk along the footpath on the side of the road, past the front of the Apostolic Church and the Park Gate Pumping Station.

6. Turn left into New Road and then left again into the Albury Estate, through the main gates. Follow the road to the Saxon Church at the far end. This church is well worth a visit and is open every day for visitors.

7. Retrace your steps to where you left the tarmac road and then head diagonally across the grass to your left and seek out the footpath sign. This sign is near the edge of a wood in an open field.

8. Take the kissing gate on the left, about 200 yards up the footpath, which enters the wood. Follow the path through the woods. The path bears to the left and exits the wood onto a drive through a gate, past South Lodge.

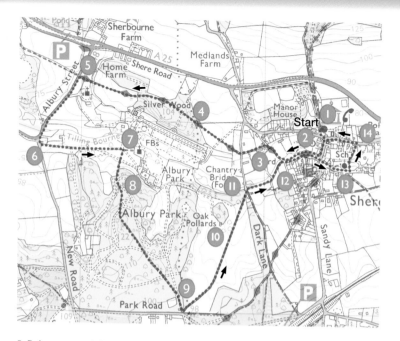

9. Before you reach Park Road, turn left through another kissing gate onto a path between the fence and the field. You almost feel you are doubling back on yourself.

10. Follow the avenue of impressive old chestnut trees and specimen oaks down the valley back towards Shere.

11. At the path junction, turn left and then right through 'Vicky's Gate' into a field running beside the Tillingbourne stream.

12. Follow the path back to the ford on Lower Street that you crossed on your outward journey and head back to the centre of the village. Cross over the square by the White Horse pub and head towards St James's Church. Take time to explore the interior.

13. Exit via the wooden gate in the graveyard on the left, behind the church. Cross the bridge and follow the path to Gomshall Lane.

14. Turn left along the road, past Shere Museum and the Village Hall, then back to the start.

DISCOVER THIS ATTRACTIVE GEORGIAN MARKET TOWN, WITH THE CASTLE TOWERING ABOVE IT, ON THIS EASY TWO-MILE STROLL. FARNHAM BECAME A WEALTHY MARKET TOWN DURING GEORGIAN TIMES, ALTHOUGH MANY OF THE BUILDINGS ARE OLDER, WITH GEORGIAN FACADES ADDED TO GENTRIFY THEM.

The largest town in Waverley Borough and one of the five largest conurbations in Surrey, Farnham is now well known for its popular summer entertainment by the river in the Gostrey Meadows and has a growing reputation as a craft town. The Maltings, a popular Arts Centre, is based here, and well worth a visit. There are also several other commercial galleries in the town.

Farnham Castle was founded in 1138 by Bishop Henry of Blois, Bishop of Winchester, the grandson of William the Conqueror. The castle became the home of the bishops of Winchester for over 800 years. The castle is now a conference and wedding venue. The castle keep is managed by English Heritage and is open to the public with free access.

Many famous authors are closely connected with, or lived in, the Farnham area including J.M. Barrie, Jonathan Swift, Alfred Lord Tennyson and Sir Arthur Conan Doyle. The author William Cobbett (the founder of Hansard, author of *Rural Rides*, MP and political reformer) is buried in a tomb just outside St Andrew's main church doors.

The Lion and Lamb Yard derives its name from a hotel of that name that once stood there. The old cellar doors are still visible near an old water pump. Much of the yard was built in the mid-1980s. It is an attractive, safe area for children, with a café in the courtyard and an impressive wooden sculpture of a lion and a lamb. Farnham Town Council office houses the local visitor information centre and is open on weekdays.

THE BASICS

Distance: 2 miles / 3.2km

Gradient: Most of the walk is flat but there is a long steady climb up to the castle

Severity: Easy

Approx. time to walk: 1½ hours but allow longer as there is so much to stop and see

Stiles: None

Maps: OS Landranger 186 (Aldershot & Guildford); OS Explorer 145 (Guildford & Farnham)

Path description: Mainly tarmac pavements and footpaths. Some well-maintained footpaths in the park, which may be muddy in the winter

Start point: Farnham railway station (GR SU 844465)

Parking: Farnham station car park* (GU9 8AD). This is often full and very expensive on weekdays, but has only a small fee for all-day parking at weekends. Other car parks are available in the town at reasonable charges

Dog friendly: Yes, but will need to be on a lead in the town due to the busy roads

Public toilets: At the railway station and several locations in the town

Nearest food: There are lots of cafés, pubs and restaurants in the town to choose from

5 FARNHAM WALK

THE ROUTE

1. The walk starts from Farnham railway station. Follow the road down to the A31. Pass the newly installed North Downs Way sculpture. Cross the road into South Street and continue along it. Go past the Town Council office and on up to The Borough.

2. Turn left into The Borough. Go past Borelli Yard and then cross over the road when you get to Castle Street.

3. Continue up Castle Street until you see the footpath on the right, signposted to Farnham Castle and Farnham Park.

4. Follow this path up to explore Farnham Castle. You can visit the castle keep, managed by English Heritage (open every day).

5. Continue on around the corner to visit Farnham Park (with children's playground).

6. Return back the way you came, down Castle Street, and look for a footpath on your right signposted 'Long Garden Walk'.

7. The footpath will veer to the left and come in at the back of Lion and Lamb Yard.

8. Leave the Lion and Lamb Yard via the front entrance with West Street. Turn right.

9. Follow West Street until you see Willmer House (now The Museum of Farnham and well worth a visit) on the other side of the road.

10. Cross over the road and return along the other side, back towards Lion and Lamb Yard. At the pedestrian crossing turn right into Church Passage into the grounds of St Andrew's Church.

11. Take the lower exit towards the river and follow the footpath beside Lower Church Lane.

12. Turn right at the Ashgate Gallery and follow the path to Gostrey Meadow.

13. At the junction with South Street, turn right and return to the railway station.

6 CHILWORTH

On this three-mile walk you will explore the fascinating ruins of a once-thriving gunpowder factory and climb to one of the highest points on the North Downs Way to enjoy spectacular views over the Tillingbourne Valley. On the way look out for alpacas, a vineyard, World War ll pillboxes and a giant wooden snail.

The Tillingbourne Valley is a tranquil, rural idyll, sited only a stone's throw from the busy market town of Guildford. It is surprising to learn that, until the late 1800s, it was one of the most industrialised valleys in the country and was exporting products all around the world. The most important of these exports was the gunpowder made at the extensive Chilworth Gunpowder Mills. First established in 1626 by the East India Company, it did not fully close until 1920. Further back in history, both a fulling and a corn mill existed at the Lower Works (the latter recorded in the Domesday Book).

The Postford Mills are best known for their 19th-century paper production. They began by producing banknote paper in 1809 and flourished until their decline in the second half of the century. In 1909, Bottings Corn Mill was constructed, which continued in operation until 1991.

High on the hill behind is St Martha's Church, on the North Downs Way National Trail. There is evidence that this church was a stopping point for pilgrims on the way to Canterbury Cathedral. In 1763, St Martha's church tower was said to have been destroyed by a massive explosion at the Gunpowder Works. Another great explosion, which killed six men, was recorded in 1901. Much of this 12th-century church was rebuilt in 1848. The church is open for visits at weekends and by appointment.

Pete Lambert

During World War II the Pillbox Line was established along the Tillingbourne Valley, designed as a final line of defence to protect London had the German army invaded from the South. If you look around on your walk you will spot abandoned tank defences and several pillboxes. For more details on this area see www.tillingbournetales.co.uk

THE BASICS

Distance: 3 miles / 5km

Gradient: One very steep hill to climb and descend

Severity: Moderate

Approx. time to walk: 2 hours

Stiles: Four

Maps: OS Landranger 186 (Aldershot & Guildford); OS Explorer 145 (Guildford & Farnham)

Path description: Variety of country footpaths and bridleways, some next to the river, which can be muddy and uneven at times. Watch out for trip hazards like tree roots

Start point: Chilworth railway station (GR TQ 031472)

Parking: No dedicated car park, but parking is available on the main road (GU4 8NP)

Dog friendly: Yes, although fields in the area contain llamas and other livestock, so leads are necessary

Public toilets: No. The only toilets on this walk are at the Percy Arms in Chilworth.

Nearest food: The Percy Arms. Several other pubs within a short drive

6 CHILWORTH WALK

THE ROUTE

1. From Chilworth railway station, make your way past Chilworth C of E Infants School. At the corner of the school is a footpath signpost, also signed 'Vera's Path'.

2. Follow this path and cross over the footbridge into the Gunpowder Works and picnic area.

3. Turn right onto the path by the picnic tables. This used to be the route of a tramway through the works. Follow the path as it veers right and runs along New Cut stream. By the stream you will spy a giant wooden snail. You will then come to the Incorporating Mills on your left. Continue on this path until you reach a gate (and the Eastern end of Middle Works).

4. Turn right onto the road and cross the stile on the opposite side, over into the field. Take the small path diagonally across the fields, crossing the stile at the other end. Then cross the second field, following the left side of the ditch. As you look left, you will see a row of triangular roofs among the trees, which were part of the Admiralty cordite works.

5. Cross the stream at the stile and footbridge, following the path between the fences to Postford Pond. Looking left, you can see a small pond with the remains of more of the works on the far shore.

6. At the road junction at the corner of the pond, turn left and follow around its left side. Note the mill channel on the left as you cross over the water. Carry on with the pond on your right.

7. As the road continues to Waterloo Pond (bending to the left), take the right path (with the pond on the left and the Tillingbourne stream on the right).

8. At the junction (A248), turn left onto the drive signed footpath, past the house, with the pond on your left. Then take the paved path into a front garden, which is a right of way. Follow the slab path through the garden and past the greenhouse to the back of the garden. Carry on following the path into the woods, over the stile.

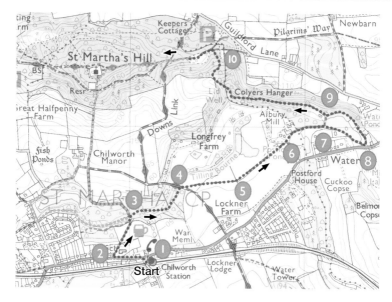

9. At the end of the path, turn right onto the plank path, passing a house on your left. Follow the path through the woods, with the Tillingbourne stream and Gunpowder Works below you. The path climbs steadily up the hill, eventually tuning into a sandy track, which will end at a junction at the top with the North Downs Way (NDW) National Trail.

10. Turn left and follow the NDW path, passing the World War II pillbox (part of the North Downs defence line).

7 DORKING

This easy, flat, two-mile walk takes you around one of Surrey's prettiest historic market towns, nestling in the stunning North Downs. The town is well known for its antiques and home to Denbies, the largest vineyard in England.

Dorking appears in the Domesday Book of 1086 as the Manor of Dorchinges. Earlier in Roman times, it was a small staging post between London and Chichester on Stane Street. The rolling chalk hills of the North Downs are on the same geological chalk belt that runs under the English Channel and across to the famous Champagne region of France. There is evidence that the Romans cultivated grape vines during their occupation of Britain. Many vineyards once again flourish in this area. Denbies, based just outside Dorking, is England's largest wine estate and was established in 1986. Its award-winning wines are now available in many supermarkets. The vineyard is well worth a visit while you are in the area as it has a café, restaurant, shop, vine tour on a little train and wine-tasting experiences.

Dorking is famous for a rare breed of chicken, which unusually has five claws. It was a favourite eating bird of Queen Victoria. A giant silver statue of this famous fowl is sited on one of Dorking's main roundabouts.

One of the original American forefathers, William Mullins (c.1572–1621), was born in Dorking. He and his family travelled as passengers on the historic 1620 voyage to America on the Pilgrim ship *Mayflower*. He was a signatory to the Mayflower Compact. His house in Dorking is the last remaining home in England still standing with links to these pilgrims.

Thomas Cubitt (1788–1855) was a famous English master builder, who developed many of the historic streets and squares of London, including Belgravia, Pimlico and Bloomsbury. He was also responsible for the east front of Buckingham Palace and involved in the redevelopment of Osborne House on the Isle of Wight. He was also responsible for building nearby Ranmore Church, using exquisite marble from around the world. The church is often referred to as the 'Cathedral in the Woods', and is well worth a visit.

The composer Ralph Vaughan Williams (1872–1958) lived and wrote music in Dorking for much of his life and penned most of the works that made him famous here. *The Lark Ascending* is perhaps his best-known work and one of the world's most recognisable and popular pieces of modern classical music. Writer Daniel Defoe, of *Robinson Crusoe* fame, attended Rev. James Fisher's boarding school in Pixham Lane, Dorking. He later mentioned the town in his journal of his tour of Great Britain.

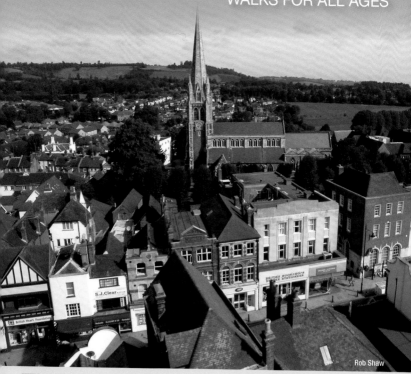

Rob Shaw

THE BASICS

Distance: 2 miles / 3.2 km

Gradient: Flat

Severity: Easy walk, much of it on tarmac pavements. One moderately inclined hill.

Approx. time to walk: 1 hour

Stiles: None

Maps: OS Landranger 187 (Dorking & Reigate); OS Explorer 146 (Dorking, Box Hill & Reigate)

Path description: Much of the walk is on flat tarmac paths

Start point: South door of St Martin's Church, Dorking (GR TQ 165494)

Parking: There are several town car parks nearby, which are reasonably priced and free on Sundays (RH4 1DW)

Dog friendly: Yes, although due to being in a town, best kept on a lead for much of the walk

Public toilets: At the Dorking Halls and the car park behind St Martin's shopping centre

Nearest food: There are lots of places to eat and drink in Dorking, including Mullins Café, the former home of Mayflower Pilgrim William Mullins, at 58 West Street

7 DORKING WALK

THE ROUTE

1. From St Martin's Church, take the path into the High Street and turn left.

2. Take the pedestrian crossing to the opposite side of the road, turning left down the broad High Street. To your left you will see the green hills of the North Downs and the slopes of Denbies vineyard, with its rows of picturesque vines. You will pass the White Horse Hotel, which is over 400 years old.

3. Turn right and progress along Dene Street.

4. Turn left up Heath Hill. The road opens out onto Cotmandene. This common land provides fine views towards Box Hill and the spire of St Martin's. Follow the trail and bear left into Moores Road. The high brick walls here once enclosed the kitchen garden of Deepdene Estate, a picturesque landscape centred on Deepdene House. The house was demolished in 1969 but the landscape is being restored.

5. Turn right at the petrol station. Outside the entrance to Dorking Halls a bronze statue celebrates the composer Ralph Vaughan Williams. Cross Reigate Road where a statue of famous Victorian builder and local resident Thomas Cubitt can be seen. You may wish to walk a few hundred yards to the Deepdene roundabout to see one of the town's more unusual statues – a giant five-toed 'Dorking cockerel'. This special breed of fowl is the symbol of the town and was supposedly introduced by the Romans. Return back along Reigate Road the trail then passes Pippbrook House, built as a private house and designed by Sir George Gilbert Scott in 1856.

6. Turn into Old London Road, crossing with care opposite Pippbrook Mill. This corn mill was one of several along the banks of the Pippbrook stream. It fell into disuse in the 16th century but was rebuilt again in the 18th century. A narrow path beyond the mill leads along the side of the mill pond.

7. Turn left along a narrow bridge into Wathen Road. A blue plaque on the left side of the street identifies the birthplace of Sir Laurence Olivier, one of Britain's most celebrated actors. Back into the High Street turn right. The shops here represent the late 19th-century expansion of the retail heart of the town, including the

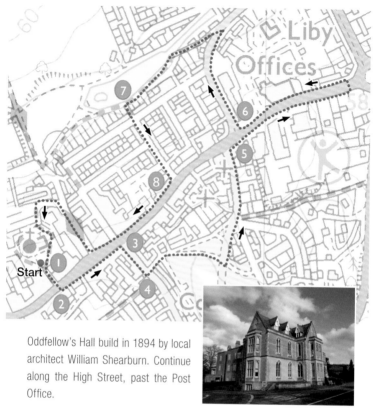

Oddfellow's Hall build in 1894 by local architect William Shearburn. Continue along the High Street, past the Post Office.

8. Turn into the modern shopping centre of St. Martin's Walk, under the projecting clock tower. At the back of the centre is a path that leads into the churchyard and back to your starting point.

8 BOX HILL

DISCOVER ONE OF THE MOST POPULAR SITES IN SURREY AND THE LOCATION OF A FAMOUS SCENE FROM JANE AUSTEN. ENJOY THE VIEWPOINTS, EXPLORE THE HISTORIC HILL FORT AND PICNIC AREA, AND VIEW THE MOST CHALLENGING PART OF THE 2012 OLYMPIC ROAD CYCLE RACE.

Box Hill takes its name from the ancient box woodland found on the steepest west-facing chalk slopes. It is estimated nearly a million people visit Box Hill each year. Jane Austen famously wrote about a picnic at Box Hill in her novel *Emma*: 'They had a very fine day for Box Hill … Nothing was wanting but to be happy when they got there. Seven miles were travelled in expectation of enjoyment, and everybody had a burst of admiration on first arriving.'

The Box Hill Fort is one of 13 mobilisation centres (known collectively as the London Defence Positions) built in the 1890s to protect London from invasion from Continental Europe. The six-acre site of the fort was originally purchased by the Ministry of Defence in 1891, and construction began in 1896. There are also extensive remains of the defences constructed during World War II for you to discover at Box Hill.

Box Hill was a focal point for the 2012 Olympic Road Cycle race and remains a mecca for cyclists to this day. There has been a café at the foot of the hill since the 1920s. It is still a family business, 'run by bikers for bikers', and is extremely popular with motorcyclist and car clubs as well as with cyclists.

A local eccentric, Peter Labilliere, was buried head downwards in accordance with his wishes near the top of the hill in 1800. There is a memorial stone near the burial place on the western side of the hill. The 17 stepping stones over the river are a very unusual historic feature. During World War II they were removed as an anti-invasion precaution, before being restored and dedicated after the war by prime minister Clement Atlee.

iStock

THE BASICS

Distance: 3 miles / 5km

Gradient: Very steep at start of walk, with steps and uneven terrain, which can get slippery in wet conditions

Severity: Moderate. Woodland paths can be uneven. Watch out for trip hazards such as tree roots. The path up Box Hill is extremely steep

Approx. time to walk: Allow 2½ hours for this challenging walk

Stiles: None

Maps: OS Landranger 187 (Dorking & Reigate); OS Explorer 146 (Dorking, Box Hill & Reigate)

Path description: Variety of footpaths, lanes and country footpaths, some next to the river

Start point: Ryka's Café, Mickleham (GR TQ 171520)

Parking: Large free car park but very popular so get there early (RH5 6BX)

Dog friendly: Yes, on a lead as there is livestock grazing in the area

Public toilets: At Ryka's Café and at the National Trust café at the top of Box Hill

Nearest food: Ryka's CAFÉ at start of walk and Box Hill Café at top of Box Hill. Nearby Stepping Stones Pub, Westhumble, is popular with walkers and welcomes dogs

iStock

THE ROUTE

1. From the car park turn left and follow the road until you see the signpost for the Zig Zag Road and Box Hill. Turn right onto the white chalk bridleway. Stay on this bridleway, which leads you up one side of the Burford Spur and takes you past the Box Hill Fort and on to the Box Hill shop and National Trust car park.

2. From the Box Hill café, follow the signs to Salomons Memorial and the spectacular viewpoint.

3. From there take the flight of steps to the footpath below. Turn right and follow this path.

4. Go through the trees and you will come out into a clearing. To your left you will see twelve concrete anti-tank obelisks along the bank of the River Mole. Continue along the path, through the trees and then left down the steps, following the North Downs Way signs. Follow this path as it descends down the hill.

5. Follow the North Downs Way descent, passing a stone sign directing you to the Stepping Stones and footbridge. Take the left fork towards the Stepping Stones.

6. Cross over the river on the seventeen stones. Head up to a car park. From there, take the left-hand fork back towards the footbridge. Do not cross the bridge, but turn left through the gate, entering Burford Meadow. Follow the path along the river bank to the A24. Take the footpath on the right alongside the A24 turning right off the A24 at the Burford Bridge roundabout, pass in front of the Burford Bridge Hotel and continue on this footpath until it stops. Cross over the road to the footpath on the other side, which ends up back at Ryka's Café.

9 NORTH DOWNS WAY

ENJOY THIS FOUR-MILE LINEAR WALK ALONG A WELL-SIGNPOSTED NATIONAL TRAIL THROUGH THE SURREY HILLS, A TRAIL ONCE TRAVERSED BY PILGRIMS ON ROUTE TO CANTERBURY CATHEDRAL. RETURN TO YOUR START POINT BY BUS OR TRAIN.

The North Downs Way (NDW) National Trail offers walkers 153 miles (246km) of spectacular scenery, picturesque villages and glorious rolling countryside, passing through the Surrey Hills and Kent Downs Areas of Outstanding Natural Beauty. The route runs from Farnham in the west of the county through Guildford, Dorking and Reigate and on to Oxted. It then travels along this ancient chalk ridge to Canterbury and Dover.

There is a dedicated team looking after the North Downs Way. The Trail is funded by Natural England and Kent and Surrey county councils. The Public Rights of Way Teams in Kent and Surrey look after the physical maintenance of the path. The North Downs Way is one of the 15 National Trails in England and Wales. National Trails are waymarked with a distinctive acorn symbol.

The NDW and the Pilgrims' Way are often said to be the same thing, but although they do intertwine they are mostly separate. The Pilgrims' Way runs between Winchester and Canterbury, often along the bottom of the Downs. In the Victorian era, much of the route became established as roads and is, these days, filled with traffic and so is less enjoyable for walking.

The walk gradually climbs along the NDW until it reaches picturesque St Martha's Church, perched high on the hill, overlooking the Tillingbourne Valley with views to the South Downs. This church was first mentioned in the Domesday Book and may have been visited by pilgrims on their journey to Canterbury. It was sympathetically renovated in Victorian times. The walk passes through the now ruined remains of Chilworth Gunpowder Mills. Once a major industrial site, it is now a quiet oasis, noted for its colony of dormice. It is also registered as a Scheduled Ancient Monument and is a Site of Special Scientific Interest.

THE BASICS

Distance: 4 miles / 6.4km

Gradient: One very steep hill to climb and to descend again at St Martha's

Severity: Moderate

Approx. time to walk: 2 hours

Stiles: None

Maps: OS Landranger 186 (Aldershot & Guildford); OS Explorer 145 (Guildford & Farnham)

Path description: Wide, well-signposted path for most of the trail. Narrow woodland paths on the Downs Link, with potential trip hazards from tree roots and rocks

Start point: Guildford Town Bridge, Guildford (GR SU 995495) (GU2 4AJ)

Finishing point: Chilworth railway station (GR TQ 030472) (GU4 8NP)

Parking: Guildford: No dedicated car parking, but parking available in the town centre. Chilworth: Leave your car at the free car park in Chilworth and then take train to Guildford to start *

Dog friendly: Subject to public transport rules

Public toilets: Several public toilets in the town and also at Shalford Sports Fields. There are no public toilets at the end of this walk, but there are toilets at the Percy Arms pub in Chilworth

Nearest food: The Percy Arms pub in Chilworth or lots of choice upon your return to Guildford

*Or you can of course start in Chilworth and simply follow the route instructions in reverse

10 THURSLEY

Discover this fabulous watery world in the west of the county, on this easy two-mile walk. It is home to a wide variety of dragonflies and damselflies, and rare heathland bog plants.

Thursley shares a Saxon and Norse heritage and is said to be named after the god Thor. This corner of Surrey has a strong war connection. During the Second World War, Allied troops trained here for D-Day on the commons. The Ministry of Defence is still active here and there is a military training camp in the area.

Thursley Common's boggy heathland is considered to be one of the best examples of acidic bogland in the south-east of England and at 326 hectares one of the largest remaining fragments of heathland. Located in the borough of Waverley, Thursley National Nature Reserve is one of the largest and most important areas of heath in Surrey. It includes areas of marsh, woodland and rare lowland heath and provides an important habitat for endangered woodlarks and Dartford warblers.

The area is also particularly noted for its range of dragonflies and damselflies. The wet areas of the reserve support 26 species, varying in size from dainty damsels and demoiselles to chunky broad-bodied chasers. The large red damselfly is usually the first to be seen, appearing in the second half of April. By midsummer there will be spring-green southern hawkers hunting alongside the sky-blue of emperors, or the yellow stripes of the golden-ringed dragonflies.

Butterflies also thrive on the common, with elusive species including purple emperors. The reserve is especially notable for its population of silver-studded blue butterflies, whose caterpillars feed on the young bell heather shoots. The sandy soils of the dry heath are home to many solitary bees and wasps.

The boggy areas support populations of one of England's largest spiders – the raft spider. The female can grow up to 22mm long (excluding legs!); both sexes are dark brown with white stripes down each side of their body. The area is also noted for several varieties of carnivorous plants.

Rare breed cattle such as Belted Galloways are used to graze this wet ground. The cattle help reduce encroaching scrub and overly dominating rough grasses such as purple moor grass. During a heatwave in July 2016 over half the common was burnt and the fire made the national news.

THE BASICS

Distance: 2 miles / 3.2 km

Gradient: Flat

Severity: Easy

Approx. time to walk: 1 hour but allow longer as there is so much to stop and see

Stiles: None

Maps: OS Landranger 186 (Aldershot & Guildford); OS Explorer OL33 (Haslemere & Petersfield)

Path description: Wide, sandy paths. Much of the walk is along well-maintained boardwalks over the water

Start point: The Moat car park, Thursley Road, Thursley (GR SU 899415)

Parking: The Moat car park (free), Thursley Road, Thursley (GU8 6LW)

Dog friendly: Yes, but keep them on leads due to nesting birds in the spring and grazing cattle in the summer and to stop them falling from the boardwalk

Public toilets: No, but there are several pubs within a short distance by car

Nearest food: The 17th-century Woolpack pub or The Mill at Elstead, a rustic pub with wooden beams and flagstone floors in a renovated 17th-century mill building are both within 5 minutes' drive

10 THURSLEY WALK

THE ROUTE

1. Go left from Moat Car Park around the lake until you come to a path on the left signposted 'Natural England Heath Trail'. Turn left along the path and onto the boardwalk. Continue on these boarded planks over the bog until you see a boardwalk path off to the right.

2. Turn right onto the side boardwalk which leads to a little island in the bog of Scots pine. The path continues over another boardwalk until you reach a T-junction.

3. Turn left here and proceed around the side of a small hill (on the right), ignoring a small path ascending the hill, and then branch right where the track splits in two, near a 'Natural England' sign. Continue along this path until it meets with a large track labelled 'Public Bridleway'.

4. Turn right walk on this path for about a quarter of a mile, before meeting a major path at a T-junction.

5. Turn right again along a larger track, which will eventually take you back to the starting point.

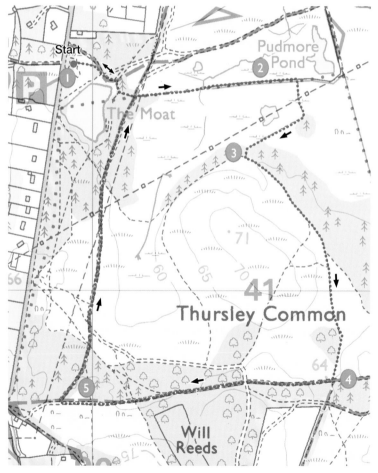

11 WOLDINGHAM

THIS EASY THREE-AND-A-HALF-MILE WALK TAKES YOU UP THE HILL FROM WOLDINGHAM RAILWAY STATION TO A GARDEN VILLAGE BUILT FOR HEROES AFTER WORLD WAR II.

The Caterham Valley is one of a number of dry valleys which run north to south across the line of the North Downs and are thought to have been cut by north-flowing rivers after the last Ice Age. The walk traverses several attractive late Victorian and early 20th-century housing estates developed after the railway was built in 1884.

Woldingham Garden Village was built originally to house the Public Schools Battalion of the Middlesex Regiment, but as the casualties mounted it was converted into a convalescent camp. The bungalow called Funny Neuk was home to the Czechoslovak military intelligence radio station from 1940 to 1942 and was used for communications concerning the assassination of the Nazi officer Reinhard Heydrich. The founder of the Garden Village was scrap merchant Henry Fuller Morris, who built 'Homes for Heroes' after the war. Some of these bungalows still stand to this day.

The Marsden Park estate was created in the 17th century by wealthy London banker and Lord Mayor of London, Sir Robert Clayton. The house is now part of Woldingham School.

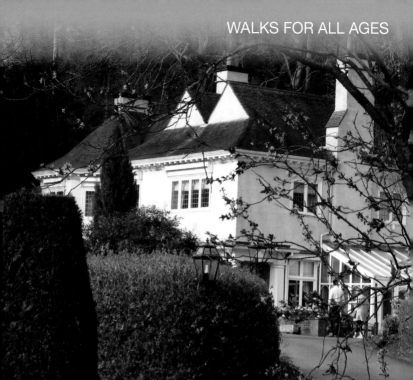

THE BASICS

Distance: 3½ miles / 5.6km

Gradient: Some gradual ascents and descents

Severity: Easy

Approx. time to walk: 1½ hours

Stiles: None

Maps: OS Landranger 187 (Dorking & Reigate); OS Explorer 146 (Dorking, Box Hill & Reigate)

Path description: Variety of pavements and country footpaths

Start point: Woldingham railway station (GR TQ 359563)

Parking: Station car park is a busy commuter car park Monday to Saturday. Free on Sundays. Some short-term parking available (with consideration) in nearby residential streets (CR3 7LT)

Dog friendly: Yes

Public toilets: Only at Dene's Garden Centre

Nearest food: Sadly, Woldingham does not have a pub! However, it does have the Dene Coffee Shop at Knight's Garden Centre

11 WOLDINGHAM WALK

THE ROUTE

1. The walk starts from Woldingham station. Leave via the front entrance, at the car park, and walk straight ahead uphill using the right-hand pavement of Station Road. Turn right up a tall flight of steps and at the top bear left and follow the tarmac path till you reach a junction with a road. Turn left and continue through the attractive Victorian residential estate. At the end of Park View Road turn left for a short downhill section until you reach a T-junction with Station Road.

2. Cross over the road and turn right. After the property called Sunnyside turn left to join a narrow footpath. At the end of this path you will come to a road. Opposite you will see two paths. Take the left-hand path and

follow this for half a mile, passing first houses and then woodland. The path is known as Madeira Walk and there are some excellent views towards London. You will come to a small section of fencing at a signed junction of paths. Keep straight ahead on the path between the fences until you emerge at crossroads. Do not take the footpath that continues opposite but instead turn right along the residential road.

3. You are now in Woldingham Garden Village. Follow the main tarmac road around the Garden Village, swinging left, then left again, then right, then left, ignoring any footpaths signed to the sides. After passing property number 1, you will come to a T-junction with Hilltop Walk. Turn right and follow the road for just 100 yards to draw level with the property called High Shaw on the left.

4. Turn right to join the signed public bridleway which leads downhill. At the bottom you will come to a road junction, with the golf course ahead of you. Turn left along Park Ley Road for about 50 yards, then fork right down the bridleway to a T-junction with Woldingham Road.

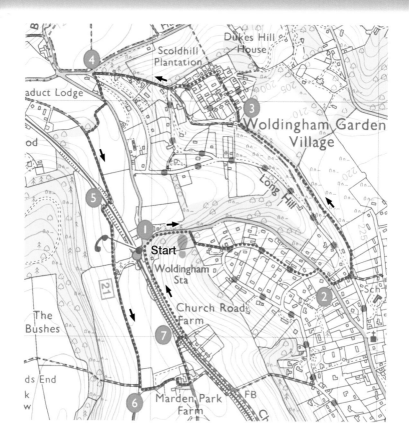

5. Turn left along the pavement but quickly turn right onto a bridleway signed to Gatwick and Redhill. At the end you will emerge at the access road to Woldingham School. Turn left along this. Follow the driveway as it swings right to reach a railway bridge and stay on the drive as it swings left.

6. Continue along the driveway and then take the first bridleway signed on the left which leads you to Marston Park. You will come to a property called Shires. Go through the gap just to the right of this property and follow the path alongside the hedge until you reach a T-junction.

7. Turn left and follow the main track passing between farm buildings and a fenced field. The lane swings right, leading you over a railway bridge, and then swings left to run parallel to the railway line down to the left. At the end of Church Road you will come to Woldingham station on the left, where you began.

Enjoy this undulating three-mile walk, discovering the wonderful rolling chalk grasslands of Farthing Down and Happy Valley. The area is owned and managed by the City of London Corporation and has stunning panoramic views over to the capital.

Farthing Downs and Happy Valley are Sites of Special Scientific Interest (SSSIs) because they form part of the largest area of chalk grassland habitat remaining in the Greater London area, which enjoys Scheduled Ancient Monument status to protect the Saxon burial mounds, Celtic field boundaries and Neolithic trackways. It has stunning panoramic views across the surrounding countryside and all the way to London. As an SSSI, it offers a safe haven to endangered wildlife and rare flowers.

Happy Valley is owned and managed by Croydon Council. Dormice and white admiral butterflies can be found in the ancient woodland. Many chalk-loving orchids grow in the rich chalk grassland, where you can find up to 50 different kinds of wild flower in late spring and summer – a beautiful sight.

The Friends of Farthing Downs is a local group run by volunteers who work to promote and protect the site. They were formed in 2005 and have been involved in numerous projects touching on all aspects of the Downs. These includes an archaeological survey in 2006, the re-planting of a beech tree in the Folly as part of the restoration of this 18th-century feature, sponsorship of new Information Boards and reprinting of the Nature Trail booklet.

THE BASICS

Distance: 3 miles / 4.8 km

Gradient: Gentle slopes

Severity: Moderate, with several declines and ascents

Approx. time to walk: 2 hours

Stiles: None

Maps: OS Landranger 187 (Dorking & Reigate); OS Explorer 146 (Dorking, Box Hill & Reigate)

Path description: Well-signposted but hilly trail, with well-signposted path for most of the trail. Some narrow woodland paths, with potential trip hazards from tree roots and rocks. The chalk surface can be slippery in wet weather

Start point: Farthing Downs car park on Ditches Lane near Coulsdon (GR TQ 301571)

Parking: Farthing Downs car park (free) on Ditches Lane (CR5 1DA)

Dog friendly: Yes, but keep dogs on leads in the summer months due to the livestock

Public toilets: Yes, in the car park

Nearest food: The Fox Pub in Old Coulsdon is nearby

12 FARTHING DOWNS
AND HAPPY VALLEY WALK

THE ROUTE

1. From the car park, cross over Ditches Lane and walk down the grass bank opposite. Where the Farthing Down cottages end on your right, swing right to the obvious level chalk path, past a vehicle barrier. Keep ahead on this main path through woodland, ignoring any side paths. You are now in Happy Valley, comprising areas of chalk grassland and ancient woodland, which gives a wonderful carpet of bluebells in the late spring. When you reach a major fork, keep left, still following the main track which descends steadily to an open area of chalk grassland. Bear slightly right along the edge of the grassland, with woodland on your right and grass sloping to the left. You may also see orchids and many types of wildflowers in these grasslands.

2. About halfway along the clearing, ignore footpaths into the woodland and continue following the right-hand edge of the clearing as it swings steadily left and downhill to a fingerpost. Turn right here, passing through a wide gap in the woodland and keep ahead, staying fairly close to the woodland edge on your left, until you reach a hedgerow crossing your path. Turn right here heading uphill so the hedgerow is on your left.

3. At the top corner, keep straight ahead to join a stone track through trees (signpost to Chaldon Church). This brings you to the edge of a large crop field. Take the obvious path diagonally left across the field. As you see woodland on your right, stay on the path to bear left, which takes you diagonally across the next section of crop field. The path leads you over the brow and heads downhill towards trees; keep on through these trees to Ditches Lane. At a fork in the lane, take the left-hand branch. The grass triangle on right is Chaldon Green, from which you can see Chaldon Church.

4. About 30 yards beyond the green, turn left onto a footpath signed Piles Wood. Go through a hedgerow gap and follow the path with the crop field (the one you just crossed) on your left. At the top right-hand corner of the crop field, continue ahead on grass track with the fence line on your right. At the end of the path you will reach a junction with a tarmac access track. Turn left on this bridleway signed Happy Valley. Stay on this path following a fence line on your right. The path descends to a junction. Keep ahead with trees on your left. At the bottom of the slope you will reach a crossroads. Turn left here and join the path along the bottom of Happy Valley.

5. Follow the valley-bottom path to the hedgerow that crosses your path (the same one as at point 3), pass through this and turn immediately right to join a smaller path leading you steeply up through woodland via steps. At the top, you will come to a T-junction. Turn left to a footpath signed to Farthing Downs. Staying on this path, you will pass benches (ideal for a refreshment break or just to enjoy a rest).

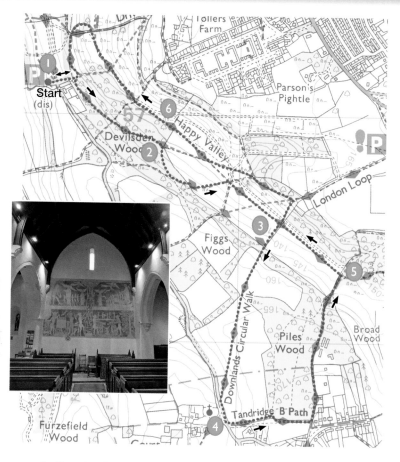

Continue ahead going downhill to eventually reach a junction of paths at the valley bottom. At the first crossroads (with a stone path running uphill to the right), go straight ahead, then fork almost immediately right and join the grass path along the valley bottom with a bench on your right.

6. At the far end of the grassland, go ahead on a wide track through trees to emerge on a narrower area of grassland. Keep straight ahead and you will soon merge with a stone path. Take this as it bears right. At the next right-hand bend on the path, turn left into a wide gap within woodland. You will reach a fork almost immediately. Take the right-hand path which heads diagonally uphill. You will enter a section of trees with a bench. Turn sharp left and follow the path uphill. Towards the top, swing right to reach the corner of Farthing Downs Cottages that you passed at the start. Dog-leg right and then left up a grass slope, with the cottages on your left. You will see the car park where you began.

13 COMPTON

This five-mile walk takes you to a magical Arts and Crafts gem hidden in the Surrey hills. Journey along the North Downs way to an artists' village, gallery and also an exquisite chapel moulded out of red clay.

This walk takes you on another section of the North Downs Way National Trail. This is a long-distance footpath through Surrey to the Kent Coast at Dover. It is 153 miles (246km) long. The route is well marked with acorn signs along its length.

The now ruined chapel of St Catherine was established in the 14th century as a chapel of ease but was abandoned by the end of the Middle Ages. It is now a Grade I listed building. The view over Guilford from this site is well worth taking your time over.

Having walked along the North Downs ridge in a westerly direction, you enter the village of Compton. One of Compton's most famous residents was the celebrated Victorian artist George Frederic Watts. Today, the Watts Gallery is dedicated to his life and work and also that of his wife, Mary Watts. Mary was much younger than her husband and upon his death she created an amazing chapel in his memory, which is open every day and free to enter. The Gallery has been kept alive by a group of dedicated volunteers. More recently it has been successful in securing a Heritage Lottery grant to renovate the gallery and purchase the artist's house across the road. There is also an interesting gift shop and café.

On your return journey look out for Polsted Manor. It is a modern house, but behind it stands the original old manor house, a small, 16th-century, timber-framed building. You will also pass through Loseley Park as you travel back towards Guildford. You will have a good view of this still privately owned, exquisite Elizabethan house, which was built in the 1500s. The house and gardens are open to the public during the summer. It is home to the present Lord Lieutenant of Surrey.

THE BASICS

Distance: 5½ miles / 9km

Gradient: Moderate, some hills to ascend and descend

Severity: Moderate

Approx. time to walk: 3 hours but allow longer as there is so much to stop and see

Stiles: None

Maps: OS Landranger 186 (Aldershot & Guildford); OS Explorer 145 (Guildford & Farnham)

Path description: Variety of footpaths, lanes and country footpaths, some next to the river and can be muddy at times

Start point: Town Bridge, Guildford (GR SU 995495), near the White House Pub (GU2 4AJ)

Parking: Park in Guildford or use the Artington Park and Ride (GU3 1LP). Free to park. Either use the bus or walk into Guildford (2½ miles along B3100)

Dog friendly: Yes, but on leads in town

Public toilets: In Guildford town and at Watts Gallery, the halfway point

Nearest food: Watts Gallery café or lots of choice on your return to Guildford. There is also the historic Withies Pub in Compton, but it is at the other end of the village on the B3000. Ye Olde Ship Inn, at St Catherine's, is on the route

THE ROUTE

1. The walk starts from the Town Bridge in central Guildford, near the White House pub. Follow the river along past the Yvonne Arnaud Theatre, where you cross a small bridge on the left. Then, before the second bridge at the canal, turn right and head along the path. Follow the canal for about a mile, until you reach the North Downs Way marker to St Catherine's – the atmospheric ruins of the old chapel, which is definitely worth the (optional) steep climb to see.

2. Turn right onto the North Downs Way and follow the markers along the ridge line towards Farnham. Walk up between the houses to the A3100, the Portsmouth Road.

3. Turn right for 50 yards and then left up Sandy Lane. After a hundred yards or so, the track bears off from the road into woodland. Follow this route along the North Downs Way for several miles until you meet Downs Lane near Watts Gallery.

4. Turn left down this road past Watts Chapel (well worth a detour) until you meet the B3000, New Pond Road.

5. Turn left and carry on along the B3000 through the pretty village of Compton (the Grade I listed 10th-century St Nicholas' Church is well worth a detour).

6. Turn left at Polsted Lane and follow it away from the main road, until you reach Polsted Manor.

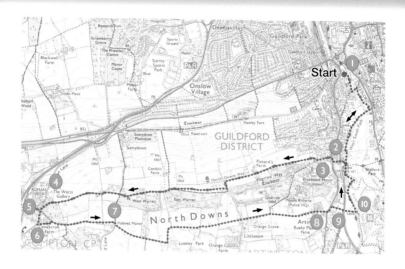

7. Take the footpath signposted to the right. Follow the path back along the lower slopes of the North Down Way for two miles. Stick to the main path, which does a dog leg about halfway along, when crossing the lovely Loseley Park estate. Eventually you reach the A3100 at Artington.

8. Walk along this road for about 200 yards.

9. Turn right down to the River Wey.

10. At the river go left and follow the path back to Guildford.

14 BANSTEAD WOODS, CHIPSTEAD

Take in the breathtaking views and varied habitat on this easy three-mile walk on the chalk downs of East Surrey. The area is famous for its rare butterflies, including the common and chalk blue, orange tip and various skippers both large and small.

Banstead Wood is an ancient semi-natural woodland with mature oaks and beech trees. In summer rare plants, including greater yellow rattle and many orchids, in particular pyramidal, common spotted, bee and fly orchids, can be seen. Many butterflies are present here, and the views are always stunning across Chipstead Valley at any time of year.

Diane Cooper

You will see marker posts dating from 1861, for a coal tax that was introduced to rebuild the City of London after the Great Fire; these posts were placed within 26 miles of the City to collect due monies. The area is now managed by Reigate and Banstead Borough Council in partnership with the Downlands Partnership. The Downlands Trust is a volunteer-run charitable trust, created in 2008 to promote in particular the aims and work of the Downlands Partnership. The Downlands Trust raises essential funds through memberships and fundraising initiatives.

Diane Cooper

THE BASICS

Distance: 3 miles / 4.8km

Gradient: Gentle hills

Severity: Moderate

Approx. time to walk: 2 hours

Stiles: None

Maps: OS Landranger 187 (Dorking & Reigate); OS Explorer 146 (Dorking, Box Hill & Reigate)

Path description: Country footpaths, some quite narrow. Watch for trip hazards like tree roots

Start point: Holly Lane car park, Chipstead (GR TQ 273583)

Parking: Holly Lane car park (free), Chipstead (CR5 3NR)

Dog friendly: Yes, but keep on a lead due to livestock

Public toilets: Nearest at 256 Coulsdon Road, Coulsdon (CR5 1EA)

Nearest food: The Ramblers Rest, Outwood Lane. The Mint public house is located on Park Road. Chipstead Station Parade has a small selection of shops and takeaway outlets

14 BANSTEAD WOODS, CHIPSTEAD WALK

THE ROUTE

1. The walk starts from the kissing gate at the rear of Holly Lane car park. Take the sloping path towards Banstead Woods, keeping to the right of the noticeboard. Keep straight ahead passing under a large yew tree. You will come to a choice of three paths ahead. On the right you will see a way marker post with yellow bands, a number one and a green-white-brown tree trunk waymark symbol with the words Banstead Woods Nature Trail. This is the first of the series of 17 posts that this nature trail follows.

2. Take the middle of three paths, which passes immediately to the left of a strange-looking oak tree. Follow the path uphill. Towards the top of the slope you will see Post 2. Turn right here.

3. Further along you will come to Post 3. Keep going on the path which leads downhill and swings right to reach a crossroads at Post 4.

4. Keep going, passing between the two yellow posts, then ignore the access track immediately on the right. Keep going uphill, for just 50 yards, to reach the next crossroads with a yellow post. Turn right here and the path leads you downhill to reach Post 5. Follow the path as it swings left passing an orchard on the right. Further along you will pass Post 6 and Post 7. Continue up the hill. Go through the barrier and you will reach a zebra crossing over Elizabeth Drive. Continue on the woodland path, winding uphill, which leads you past Post 8 and on to Post 9 and 10. Keep ahead on the winding woodland path and you will come to a T-junction at Post 11. Bear right here.

5. You will come to another T-junction. Bear right and then follow the path as it swings left to reach a major crossroads. Keep straight ahead, passing Post 12 on the left. Keep going and, after just a few yards, the path leads you past Post 13. Continue on to reach Post 14 where you will find a fenced pond on the left, with some strategically placed benches, ideal for birdwatching or your picnic.

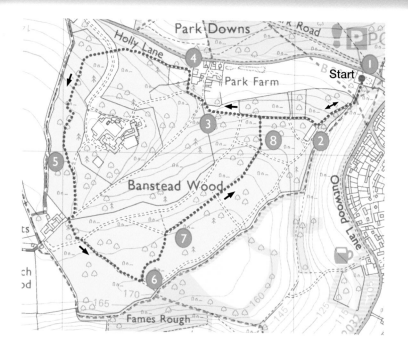

6. Turn left, passing the pond on the left. The path winds ahead to reach a junction with a way marker post. Turn sharp right here onto the smaller path, heading south once again. At the crossroads with a path, keep straight on. After just a few paces you will emerge to a T-junction with another path. Turn left for just a few yards and you will come to a fork at the edge of a more open grass section. Take the right-hand path and follow the path between young trees and scrub. The path will lead you to Post 15. Here the route continues to the left, but it is worth taking a small diversion to the right to reach a viewpoint across the valley.

7. Go back to Post 15 and continue left. At the crossroads, keep straight ahead to re-enter the ancient woodland. After just a few paces you will come to another crossroads with a large oak tree at its centre. Keep straight ahead and then, at the next major crossroads turn right.

8. The path leads you past Post 16 on the right. Keep ahead at the next crossroads, with a bench on the right. Continue to the next crossroads where you will see Post 17. Follow the main path which heads downhill. At the T-junction turn right and after about 100 yards you will come to a junction with a path on the left. Keep straight ahead to the end of the path, then turn left down the hill back to the car park.

15 HORSELL COMMON

DISCOVER THIS FOUR-MILE LOWLAND HEATH AREA, MADE FAMOUS BY SCI-FI AUTHOR H.G. WELLS IN THE WAR OF THE WORLDS. HE IMAGINED ALIENS LANDING IN A SANDPIT ON THIS COMMON, BEFORE THEY BEGAN TO WREAK HAVOC ON EARTH.

The area was once part of Windsor Great Park. It is now part of the Thames Basin Heath Environmental Management Partnership. The common is managed by volunteers, the Horsell Common Preservation Society. In 1966, they purchased the site at a price of £1 per acre. The Common covers 880 acres.

The area is a Site of Special Scientific Interest (SSSI), which gives it special planning protection, and is an example of rare lowland heathland. Less than 2 per cent of the world's lowland heaths remain and Surrey contains a substantial amount of this now rare habitat.

The author H.G. Wells (1866–1946) lived in nearby Maybury. He regularly walked on this common and planned many of his novels here. He is now best remembered for his science fiction novels and is often called 'the father of science fiction'.

On this walk you will see the headquarters of the McLaren Group (the racing car marque), which was opened in 2003. It was designed by the famous architect, Sir Norman Foster. You will also be walking by Fairoaks Airport, which was opened in 1931. It was used by the military from 1936. Over 6,000 Tiger Moth pilots trained here. Today is used as a maintenance airfield and also hosts many light aircraft.

Thanks to Woking Borough Council

THE BASICS

Distance: 4 miles / 6.4km

Gradient: Flat

Severity: Easy

Approx. time to walk: 2 hours

Stiles: None

Maps: OS Landranger 186 (Aldershot & Guildford); OS Explorer 145 (Dorking, Box Hill & Reigate)

Path description: Sandy path across heathland, grassland and woodlands

Start point: Horsell Common car park, Woking (GR TQ 012604)

Parking: Horsell Common car park (free) – close to Six Crossroads Roundabout (GU21 4HQ)

Dog friendly: Yes, although please keep dogs on leads during the spring bird breeding season

Public toilets: None

Nearest food: The Hangar Café at Fairoaks Airport, The Cricketers Pub, The Red Lion or the Water's Edge café

15 HORSELL COMMON WALK

THE ROUTE

1. The walk starts from the Horsell Common car park on the A245 near to the Six Crossroads roundabout, just north of Woking. There are several car parks on this road so make sure you park in the one closest to the roundabout. From the car park, take the path directly opposite the vehicle entrance, follow this path to the centre of the common and you will pass an information board on the left. Stay on the main path and ignore any smaller paths to the left and right.

2. When you come to a bench ahead, go through the gap in the ridge alongside it and head down a small path into an open sandy clearing.

3. From this clearing take the path heading diagonally right. Following the path ahead, you will pass the sand pits and lake to the left. Keep in the same direction and you will reach a bench carved with the name Hanning Seat.

4. Continue on and after just a short distance you will come to a T-junction – keep left here. Follow the path bending left and keep ahead past a couple of tall wooden barriers. You will come to a crossroads with more barriers – turn right here.

5. Keep ahead on this straight path and you will pass alongside two vehicle barriers. Turn left immediately after the second barrier and follow the gravel drive with houses to the right. At the end of the houses, on the stone track, head back into the common. At the next junction keep going straight ahead, passing a house to the left. A few paces later you will come to the wooden posts and notice boards marking the entrance to McLaren Park.

6. Keep on the main path through the park and soon you will get your first view of the McLaren Technology Centre. Follow the path as it now swings right, following the curve of the formal lake. As you draw level with the main building, fork left, cross a bridge over the river and through a gate. When you emerge out of the trees you will see Fairoaks Airport.

7. Keep on the path passing the windsock. Enter a section of woodland and follow this path to the T-junction with the road.

8. Turn left alongside Chertsey Road. Cross over the main entrance road for the airport.

9. Turn left into Youngstroat Lane. Follow the road onto the bridleway with the fenced horse paddocks on the right. On the left you will pass by the end of the airport runway. Cross the footbridge and go through the gate, staying on the bridleway. At the far side of the field, pass through the gate and cross over the larger wooden footbridge.

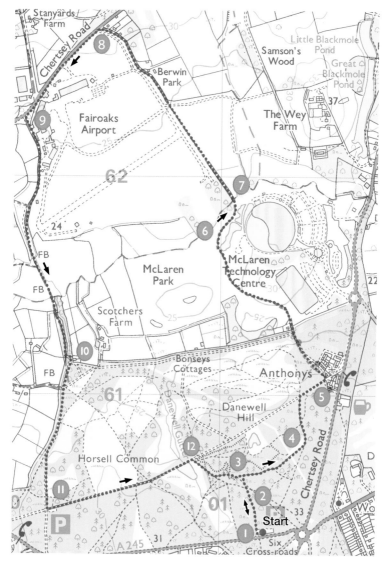

10. Follow the stone bridleway and at the end of the long straight section bear left over a small stream. This marks the re-entry point for Horsell Common.

11. Bear right onto the bridleway marked with a blue arrow. Follow this path along the edge of the common close to the fence boundary on the right. You will come to a major crossroads. Turn left here and head towards the centre of the common.

12. Turn right, just after the pond, to retrace your steps back to the car park.

16 WOTTON AND FRIDAY STREET

THIS WALK TAKES IN THE SPRAWLING WOODED PATHS AROUND THE WOTTON ESTATE. EXPLORE THE HISTORIC MILLING HAMLETS, ADMIRE THE ARCHITECTURE OF WOTTON HOUSE AND ENJOY THE ORNAMENTAL WATERFALL AT BROADMOOR, THE HIGHEST WATERFALL IN SURREY.

This walk takes you into some of the most hidden rural parts of Surrey, little changed since Norman times. The 1086 Domesday Book lists the manor of 'Wodeton', including a mill. The Manor of Wotton was conveyed to George Evelyn in 1579. The Evelyn family still own the Wotton estate to this day. They made their money from the Gunpowder Mills along the Tillingbourne Valley.

Probably the most well-known member of the family was John Evelyn, FRS (1620–1706), the writer, gardener and diarist. Evelyn's journals are largely contemporaneous with those of his fellow diarist, Samuel Pepys. They cover the time of the deaths of Charles I and Oliver Cromwell, the last Great Plague of London and the Great Fire of London in 1666.

John Evelyn was a pioneering landscape designer and his work includes the creation of mini waterfalls. He designed the Italian Garden at Wotton House in the 1640s, whose features included a temple, a mount and a fountain. Restoration and further garden developments took place in the 1860s, including deer and kangaroo paddocks.

The Mill Pond in the hamlet of Friday Street is all that remains of the former mill site here, other than the associated 17th-century cottages and mill house. The mill closed in the 1730s, quite possibly to allow for steepening the water gradient as part of John Evelyn's estate landscaping plans.

The waterfall at Broadmoor is supplied by a leat from the Tillingbourne River, constructed around 1738 by a Dutchman called Jacobsen as a set piece of the illustrious garden landscaping in the Wotton Estate. Originally, it was part of an intricate design, complete with pavilion, statues and ornamental urns. Not far from the source of the River Tillingbourne at Tilling Springs, it is Surrey's highest waterfall.

The historic Stephan Langton pub at Friday Street bears the name of the Archbishop of Canterbury during the reign of King John, a signatory of the Magna Carta. In 1984 the village was used as a location for the BBC Television series *The Tripods* based on the books by John Christopher, in which it portrayed the village of Wherton where the story begins.

THE BASICS

Distance: 3miles / 5km

Gradient: One gentle hill to ascend and descend

Severity: Moderate. Woodland paths which can be a bit uneven

Approx. time to walk: 2 hours

Stiles: Two

Maps: OS Landranger 186 (Aldershot & Guildford); OS Explorer 145 (Guildford & Farnham)

Path description: Variety of country footpaths and bridleways, some next to the river. Can be uneven and muddy in places. Watch out for trip hazards like tree roots

Start point: Wotton Village Hall car park (GR TQ 126476)

Parking: Village Hall car park (free) (RH5 6QQ)

Dog friendly: Yes, although fields in the area contain livestock, so leads are necessary when passing fields

Public toilets: No. The only toilets on this walk are at the pubs

Nearest food: Wotton Hatch at the start point and the Stephan Langton pub at the midway point. Both are very popular at weekends so best to book in advance. Also recommended is afternoon tea at Wotton House Hotel

THE ROUTE

1. From the Wotton Village Hall car park, take the path on the left side of the village hall as it runs diagonally across the field and the cross over the stile onto Wotton Drive.

2. Turn left and follow the drive towards Wotton House.

3. At the end of the hedge on the left, cross the stile and take the path on the left-hand side of the field, crossing over the Tillingbourne and into the woods. It is worth following the drive all the way down to take a look at Wotton House, now a hotel. You can visit, or have a drink there before returning to the route.

4. Follow the track along the valley to the Friday Street mill pond. The building on your left by the corner of the pond was a 16th-century corn mill. You may wish to stop for lunch at the historic Stephan Langton pub.

5. Turn left at the pond corner and follow the road (Noons Corner), with the pond on your right. Just past the pond take the small path on the right into the woods and up the hill. Continue on this path as it crosses the two roads.

6. Where the path forks, go right and downhill, cutting behind the houses.

7. Then go left downhill between the gardens, to meet the road at Broadmoor hamlet.

8. Turn left along the road, following it around the bend to the point where it forks to the right.

9. Take right path, which continues along the Greensand Way into the Wotton Estate. Carry on along the Greensand Way, past the waterfall, until you come onto a house drive and Sheephouse Lane.

10. As you approach the A25, go left and follow the road 400 yards back to the village hall car park.

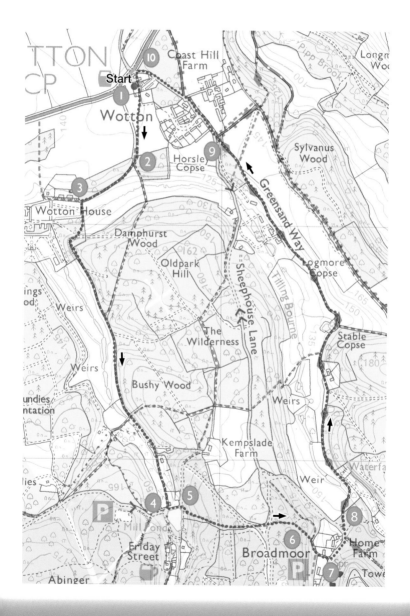

THIS IS AN EASY TWO-MILE FLAT STROLL AROUND THIS PRETTY VILLAGE AND SURROUNDING COUNTRYSIDE THAT INCLUDES A SECTION OF THE REDUNDANT RAILWAY LINE THAT RAN FROM GUILDFORD TO THE SOUTH COAST – NOW A LONG-DISTANCE WALKING TRACK CALLED THE DOWNS LINK.

Cranleigh claims to be the largest village in England. The village is not mentioned in the Domesday Book and was very small until the coming of the Wey and Arun Canal in 1816, and then the railway in 1865.

St Nicolas' Church contains a carved figure of a cat that is said to have been the inspiration for Lewis Carroll's Cheshire Cat, from *Alice in Wonderland*. Lewis Carroll did visit the church when he lived in Guildford.

The local department store, David Mann & Sons, opened in 1887 and is still in business today. Cranleigh School, an independent co-educational boarding school, is located on the outskirts of the village. It opened in 1865 and was originally known as The Surrey County School. The first cottage hospital in the country was started in Cranleigh in 1859. It has survived many attempts to close it, thanks to the fundraising efforts of the local community.

Cranleigh Arts Centre is well worth a visit. Built in 1847, it spent its first 117 years as the village school before closing in 1966. In 1985 it opened as a permanent arts centre. Originally run entirely by volunteers, today it only employs a few staff, with the majority of operations still undertaken by members of the local community.

The Cranleigh Line was a linking railway line that connected Guildford, on the Portsmouth–London line, with the West Sussex market town of Horsham and then via another line to the south coast. The line ran through Cranleigh and was just under 20 miles (31 km) in length. The line closed on 14 June 1965 only four months short of its centenary, the only Surrey railway closure in the mid-1960s under the programme that was officially termed 'The Reshaping of British Railways' but became better known as the Beeching Axe.

THE BASICS

Distance: 2 miles / 3.2 km

Gradient: Flat

Severity: Easy flat walk

Approx. time to walk: 1 hour but allow longer as there is so much to stop and see

Stiles: None

Maps: OS Landranger 186 (Aldershot & Guildford); OS Explorer 145 (Guildford & Farnham)

Path description: Variety of footpaths, lanes and country footpaths, some next to the river

Start point: Cranleigh Village Hall, Village Way, Cranleigh (GR TQ 058390)

Parking: At Cranleigh Village Hall (GU6 8AF). There is also free parking on side streets but the main town car park near the Village Hall is reasonably priced and free on Sundays

Dog friendly: Yes, but will need to be on a lead near the roads

Public toilets: Near the Village Hall and by the cricket pitch

Nearest food: Lots of choice here

17 CRANLEIGH WALK

THE ROUTE

1. The walk starts from the Village Hall which was opened in 1933. Walk to the right of the Leisure Centre to the area known as snoxhall Sports fields. Here you will meet the Downs Link path, formerly the railway line closed in 1966 as part of the Beeching cuts.

2. Turn right here and follow the path which runs behind the main High Street of Cranleigh, then past the site of the old station at Stockland Square, which is now just a large car park.

3. Keep on this path until you meet with Elmbridge Road. Turn right and walk along the edge of the common towards a roundabout and views of the main common and cricket pitch.

4. Cross over Guildford Road at the roundabout and enjoy viewing the pretty row of cottages on the green. Continue walking straight ahead into what becomes Horseshoe Lane.

5. Just after Edgefield Close on the right, take the path across Cranleigh School playing fields until you reach a T-junction with another path.

6. Turn right again and head towards Glebelands School, passing by it on your right. Cross over Parsonage Road and take the path opposite, down past Cranleigh Primary School. Eventually you arrive near St Nicolas' Church and the main road through the centre of the town.

7. Cross at the crossing near Cranleigh Art Centre. Turn right again and walk along the footpath until you reach the Village Hall again.

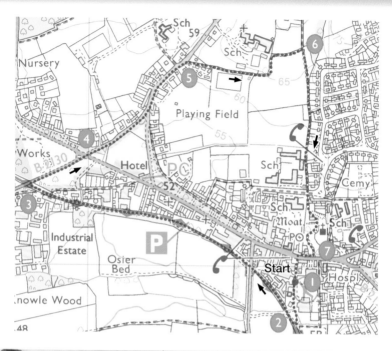

ENJOY THIS SHORT, FLAT, TWO-AND-A-HALF-MILE WALK FROM THE OLD COACHING VILLAGE OF RIPLEY, OVER THE WEY NAVIGATIONS TO PYRFORD, AND RETURN VIA THE PICTURESQUE RUIN OF NEWARK PRIORY.

Ripley has existed since Norman times. Lying on the main road approximately halfway between London and Portsmouth, it was once a popular coaching village and there are still several inns and half-timbered houses dating from Tudor and Elizabethan times. Lord Nelson was said to have meet his mistress, Emma Hamilton, here on his way to Portsmouth to join the Fleet.

Ripley was the post town for the whole area (including Woking) from 1813 to 1865. With the coming of the railway to what was then Woking Common in 1838, Ripley's importance diminished, and Woking gathered importance as the main centre for the area from this time. The village has always been popular with cyclists since Victorian times and the village green has been the scene of cricket matches since the 18th century.

The Wey Navigations were planned over three hundred years ago by Sir Richard Weston of Sutton Place, and run between Weybridge and Guildford. The original bridges and locks were built from the ruins of Oatlands Palace, near Weybridge.

The name Pyrford is derived from the Saxon Pyrianforde, which means 'the ford by the pear tree'. The area has a long history with evidence of habitation from prehistoric times. The Pyrford Stone which now stands at the corner by Upshott Lane is thought to be a prehistoric standing stone. The circular hilltop churchyard of St Nicholas' Church is indicative of an early settlement. Evidence has been found of Roman occupation, and a pot of coins from the first century AD was discovered when Romans Way was being built.

When William the Conqueror conducted the great Domesday Survey, Pyrford had a population of around a hundred. There was arable land for seven plough teams, half of which were owned by the villagers themselves, together with fifteen acres of meadows and woods with pasture for eighty pigs. Two mills were recorded and there may have been a chapel.

St Nicholas' Church is set on a knoll overlooking the ruins of Newark Priory. The church is Norman, complete and virtually unspoilt, with an original Tudor porch. The interior has a wonderful timbered roof, the pews are 15th century and the pulpit is Jacobean. Opposite the nave is a wall painting dating from 1140.

Newark Priory was founded at the end of the twelfth century by Ruald de Clane and his wife Beatrice of Send. King Henry VIII dissolved the monasteries in 1539. At Newark, the prior was pensioned off, the valuables were sent to the Tower of London and the land was given to the Master of the King's Horse. It has been said that a cannon was employed from the top of Church Hill to bombard the Priory.

The area around Pyrford Mill is the site of a prehistoric village from around 1500 BC, which was discovered in 1926. The watermill at Pyrford was burned to the ground in 1966.

THE BASICS

Distance: 2½ miles / 4 km

Gradient: Flat

Severity: Easy

Approx. time to walk: 1½ hours

Stiles: Two

Maps: OS Landranger 186 (Aldershot & Guildford); OS Explorer 145: (Guildford & Farnham)

Path description: Much of the walk is on flat paths but can get muddy

Start point: Ripley Village Green car park (GR TQ 052570)

Parking: Ripley Village Green car park (free) (GU23 6AR)

Dog friendly: Yes

Public toilets: In Ripley and at The Anchor Pub midway round the route

Nearest food: Wide variety of choice in Ripley, or at The Anchor Pub halfway through the walk

THE ROUTE

1. From the Ripley village green car park, take the wide track across the green, with the cricket pitch on your right. You will soon see a large house, Dunsborough Park, on the left. The gardens are sometimes open to the public and are especially noted for their display of tulips.

2. At the end of some farm cottages, where the track ahead is marked 'Strictly Private', bear left on a path which soon crosses Ockham Mill Stream. Then, at a house, go slightly to the left between holly bushes and over a footbridge. Continue on to the lock and weir. You may see herons on this stretch of water meadow.

3. Cross over the weir and turn right past the lock cottage. Do not go over the small footbridge but continue along the towpath, which lies between the Wey Navigation and the River Wey for a short distance.

4. Keep on the towpath for about a mile, passing attractively decorated barges and houseboats, until you reach the lock at The Anchor Pub, Pyrford.

5. Turn left at the end of the footpath and continue on a track between fields to cross a stile.

6. Continue on the track until you emerge on a road (Church Hill). Turn left up to St Nicholas' Church, Pyrford, which is set on a low knoll overlooking the ruins of Newark Priory.

7. Go through the churchyard with the church on your left, down the gravel path and out onto the road.

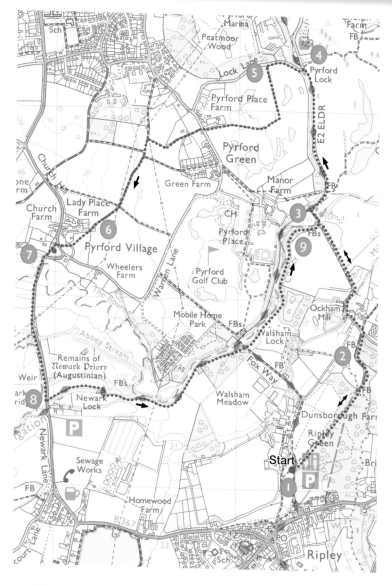

8. After about a quarter of a mile, passing the ruins on your left, walk to the traffic lights and turn left down the towpath.

9. Cross the canal at the lock and continue along the towpath. On reaching the lock and weir again, turn right and retrace the last half mile back to the starting point.

19 SHAMLEY GREEN

Enjoy a short walk around this quintessential, south of England village known for its cricket. Its famous residents include Richard Branson, Alfred Hitchcock and Winnie the Pooh illustrator, E.H. Shepard. It also has an interesting connection with cats.

Shamley Green, or Shamele as it was first referred to in a taxation list of 1332, started as a collection of small farms and houses forming an agricultural hamlet in the Parish of Wonersh. Its isolated farmsteads were located on sites carefully selected to meet the basic needs of residents for water, access, shelter, drainage and varied land use as the ancient forest cover was cleared.

From Elizabethan times through to the 18th and early 19th centuries, further developments occurred around the peripheries of the open spaces which formed the village green. Small shops and artisan activities evolved to sustain this fairly isolated, self-sufficient rural economy. Many of these buildings remain to this day, although most are now converted into houses.

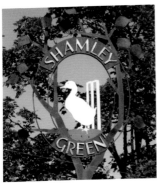

A chapel of ease built on Plonks Hill in 1863–4 became the Shamley Green Parish Church in 1881, by which time the original hamlet had become an independent village. The current church was built in 1863 by Charles Henry Howell, who was also the architect for County Hall in Kingston.

This walk is reported by locals to have been used many times by the celebrated poet T.S. Eliot, visiting for rest and relaxation during World War II. He wrote, among other things, the poems about cats that Andrew Lloyd Webber's musical is based on. Locals say an old lady lived on the hill with hundreds of cats and perhaps helped inspire Eliot to write the collection. Still on a feline theme, Shamley Green was the focus of a BBC television documentary on cats' behaviour in 2013. The village was chosen because of the high population of cats living here – one of the highest, in fact, in the country.

The world-famous film director Sir Alfred Hitchcock named his production company Shamley Productions after the village where he had lived. Other famous residents have included singer and comedian Sir Harry Secombe, artist and TV presenter Tony Hart and business tycoon Sir Richard Branson.

THE BASICS

Distance: 2 miles / 3.2km

Gradient: Easy walk with one steep hill to climb (but this can be avoided)

Severity: Easy to moderate. Woodland paths can be a bit uneven. Watch out for trip hazards like tree roots

Approx. time to walk: 1 hour

Stiles: Two

Maps: OS Landranger 186 (Aldershot & Guildford); OS Explorer 145 (Guildford & Farnham)

Path description: Variety of country footpaths, lanes and bridleways

Start point: Shamley Green cricket green (GR TQ 032439)

Parking: Free parking around the green (GU5 0UB)

Dog friendly: Yes, but be aware of livestock in the fields

Public toilets: Only in the two pubs and café

Nearest food: The Red Lion and The Bricklayers Arms, both in Shamley Green, welcome dogs and families. Also there is The Speckledy Hen café on the green

19 SHAMLEY GREEN WALK

THE ROUTE

1. This walk starts from the centre of the village. Parking can be difficult but there is some parking around the green and some in the side streets. From the green, head up past The Bricklayers Arms on the B2128 towards Cranleigh.

2. Cross over the road where the pavement runs out and turn left through an old iron kissing gate to the churchyard.

3. Turn left at the church and, once past it, you will see a gate opening onto a public footpath. Before you leave the churchyard, if you are interested, follow the hedge line down to the bottom of the churchyard to a tall white gravestone belonging to E.H. Shepard, the illustrator of the famous *Winnie the Pooh* books. He was a long-term resident of the village and many of his illustrations are from the local area. Once through the gate, turn left along the narrow footpath, which opens out between two large fields. Over to the left, on Chinthurst Hill, you will spy the last folly built in England, in the 1930s, by architect Edwin Lutyens.

4. After going through a kissing gate, continue along between two fields. The path will veer right for 200 yards before coming out on a tarmac avenue.

5. Keep right and walk down through the avenue of chestnuts.

6. At the T-junction, turn left and go down past Reel Hall, which dates back to the 17th century. A 'reel' is a small stream, which you will cross.

7. Here you meet a road – Woodhill Lane (to avoid the steep hill climb, follow this road back to the village green). Otherwise, turn left and then almost immediately right at the sign marking the bridle path. This path now ascends sharply for about 500 yards through a pretty coppiced woodland. Towards the top of the hill, you will meet a Y-junction with signposting.

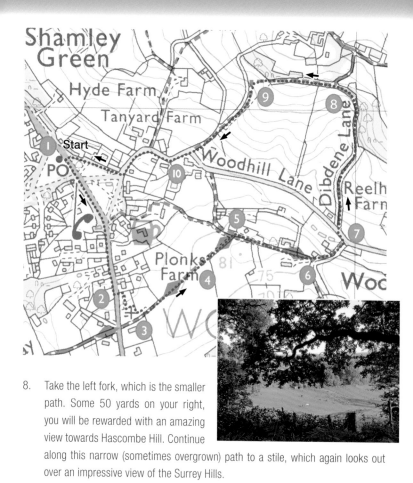

8. Take the left fork, which is the smaller path. Some 50 yards on your right, you will be rewarded with an amazing view towards Hascombe Hill. Continue along this narrow (sometimes overgrown) path to a stile, which again looks out over an impressive view of the Surrey Hills.

9. From the stile, head down the hill, following the fence line. A tarmac drive and the path merge after the next stile.

10. Turn left and, at the bottom of the hill, turn right onto Woodhill Lane. This road will take you back to the village past Tanyard Farm, childhood home of Sir Richard Branson, founder of the Virgin Group. Once on the Green look at the old forge, now the Speckledy Hen café. The large stone circle used for putting wheels together is still evident outside. Just before the café is a very attractive old house called the Courthouse. This was where a local court used to be run. The village pond contains a population of rare great crested newts.

20 RUNNYMEDE

THIS HILLY BUT EASY FOUR-MILE WALK TAKES IN THREE
INCREDIBLE MEMORIALS ALONG THE WAY: THE JOHN F.
KENNEDY, MAGNA CARTA AND AIR FORCE MEMORIALS. IT
MAKES FOR A FASCINATING FREE DAY OUT, WITH LOTS TO SEE
ALONG THE WAY.

The stone memorial to John F. Kennedy was created from a seven-ton block of Portland
stone that is thought to be around 100 million years old. The cobbled steps at the memorial
are called *The Steps of Individuality*. There are 50 steps in all, each representing one of
the states of the USA. The cobble setts are said to represent the multitude of pilgrims on
their journey to enlightenment.

The Magna Carta memorial in Runnymede was built
in 1957 to commemorate the Great Charter. It was
designed and built by famous architect Sir Edward
Maufe (who also designed The Air Force Memorial
and Guildford Cathedral). It was dedicated in a
ceremony on 28 July 1957 attended by the Queen.

Nearly 800 years ago, King John met with a group of
barons at Runnymede and sealed the Magna Carta.
This is seen by many as the symbolic first step on
the road to modern democracy. Today, in this spirit,
Runnymede has several memorials to the ongoing
struggle for liberty. Also now sited there is *The Jurors*, a public artwork permanently
situated where the Magna Carta was sealed. It was created by British artist Hew Locke
in 2015.

The Fairhaven Memorial Lodges and the land here were donated by Lady Fairhaven to the
National Trust. She commissioned Sir Edwin Lutyens to design the lodges in memory of her
husband Sir Urban Broughton MP, who had bought the land to safeguard its future. Today
you can visit South Lodge, home to the Magna Carta tearoom.

The Air Force Memorial at Englefield Green was unveiled in 1953. Over 116,000 men and
women of the Commonwealth air forces gave their lives during World War II. This memorial
is a fitting tribute to the 20,000 with no known graves. You can climb the spiral staircase
to reach a rooftop viewing platform, with magnificent views over to Windsor Castle.

THE BASICS

Distance: 4½ miles / 7 km

Gradient: Gradual descent downhill at start of walk and then again on return route. The rest of the walk is flat

Severity: Easy to moderate

Approx. time to walk: 2½ hours but allow longer as there is so much to stop and see

Stiles: None

Maps: OS Landranger 175 (Reading & Windsor); OS Explorer 160 (Windsor, Weybridge & Bracknell)

Path description: Variety of footpaths, lanes and muddy paths, some next to the river

Start point: Car park on Cooper's Hill Lane, Englefield Green (GR SU 995718)

Parking: Air Forces Memorial car park, Cooper's Hill (TW20 0LB)

Dog friendly: Yes, but be careful of cattle grazing on the Runnymede meadows

Public toilets: At the start of the walk, at National Trust Café, and also Runnymede Pleasure Grounds

Nearest food: There is the National Trust café at Runnymede halfway through the walk. Nearby Englefield Green also has a great range of cafés and pubs for after your walk

20 RUNNYMEDE WALK

THE ROUTE

1. From the car park turn left along Cooper's Lane (heading away from the sign to the Air Forces Memorial). Follow the lane all the way to the T-junction, keeping left at the fork at Priest Hill.

2. Turn right and follow the road steadily downhill. You can cross over the road to join the pavement running on the left-hand side.

3. Towards the bottom of the hill, turn right through the white gate to join the tarmac lane signed as a public footpath. This leads you steadily downhill until you reach Priest Hill Farm.

4. Keep straight ahead, passing the buildings of Priest Hill Farm on your right, to join the unmade track leading you past a National Trust 'Runnymede' sign on your left. At the junction, keep straight ahead until you meet a cobbled clearing where the J.F. Kennedy memorial is sited. Follow the cobbled steps to the bottom, go through the kissing gate into Runnymede fields and turn left to visit the 2015 Magna Carta anniversary art installation called *The Jurors* and the National Trust Visitor Centre.

5. Head back past the gate by which you entered the field, to visit the Magna Carta memorial. Then turn right for a few paces to reach the field corner. Do NOT go through the gate ahead; turn left along the field edge, towards the road with a wire fence running on your right.

6. At the road, turn right through the kissing gate and follow the edge of the field with the road running on your left. After 150 yards, turn left through the kissing gate and cross over Windsor Road. At the far side, turn right to join the Thames Path, with the River Thames on your left. Follow the path and stay with the river as it swings left leading you away from the road. On the right you will come to a statue of Queen Elizabeth II.

North Downs Way near Guildford Pete Lambert

WALKS FOR ALL AGES
SURREY